Two Plays

TWO PLAYS

The Island of Demons . *Six Dry Cakes for the Hunted*

GEORGE WOODCOCK

Vancouver · Talonbooks · 1977

published with assistance from the Canada Council

Talonbooks
201 1019 East Cordova
Vancouver
British Columbia V6A 1M8
Canada

This book was typeset by Linda Gilbert of B.C. Monthly Typesetting Service, designed by David Robinson and printed by Hemlock Printers for Talonbooks.

First printing: December 1977

Talonplays are edited by Peter Hay.

Rights to produce "The Island of Demons" and "Six Dry Cakes for the Hunted" from *Two Plays*, in whole or in part, in any medium by any group, amateur or professional, are retained by the author and interested persons are requested to apply to him at 6429 McCleery Street, Vancouver, B.C. V6N 1G5.

Canadian Cataloguing in Publication Data

Woodcock, George, 1912–
    Two plays

    Contents: The island of demons. —
Six dry cakes for the hunted.
    ISBN 0-88922-123-5

    I. Title. II. Title: The island of
demons.   III. Title: Six dry cakes for
the hunted.
PS8545.O56T96   C812'.5'4   C78-002085-5
PR9199.3.W65T96

to Gerald Newman

The Island of Demons

A Canadian Legend

Scene One

*The setting is the cabin of a fishing boat bound
from Canada to France. The year is 1545.*

CAPTAIN:
> Our prow swings east and the wind turns to France.
> In a short month your friends and kin should greet you.

MARGUERITE:
> I have no friends, sir, and for kin
> Only my dearest enemy.

CAPTAIN:
> Your dearest enemy? Whom do you mean?

MARGUERITE:
> I mean . . . no one. Nothing. . . .
> Nothing that need be spoken.
> But nothing need ever be spoken.

CAPTAIN:

> You speak in the dark always, hinting at shadows.
> You have been a week now on my ship,
> And still I do not know you,
> Who you are — where you come from —
> How you came to be where I found you.
> I might have nobody travelling on my ship.

MARGUERITE:

> I might have Nobody travelling within me.
> Life is a cipher in the mind alone
> On a shore where the past is wiped out
> Like a bird's footprints on the beach
> As the tide rises and the sea
> Makes somewhere nowhere.

CAPTAIN:

> You must have had a name at least.

MARGUERITE:

> I had a name. I listen to it now.
> It sounds like a stranger's name.
> Once I was called Marguerite . . .
> Marguerite!
> Now you know what to call me, Captain.
> I have a name like a cat or a dog.

CAPTAIN:

> Have you no more to tell me?
> The name of your family? The house and the town
> Whose walls sheltered your childhood?

MARGUERITE:

> That is all past. I do not want to remember.

CAPTAIN:

> That is always your answer. You lift it like a mask.
> Surely you remember something!
> How you came to this island . . .
> Surely you remember that!

MARGUERITE:
>I have remembered too much. . . .
>You are kind, sir . . . I know you are kind . . .
>But what I remember is better forgotten,
>Better buried with the hearts I buried. . . .

CAPTAIN:
>The hearts you buried?

MARGUERITE:
>The hearts I buried, in coffins of bone and flesh,
>And the beasts calling like demons in the woods,
>And the demons calling like beasts in the air,
>And we hiding in the house of driftwood
>On the empty shore above high tide
>And one by one by one
>The tides and the nights. . . .

>>*The light on the scene fades and the sound of waves beating on a beach rises to crescendo and fades, as the present fades into the past in the next scene.*

Scene Two

>*The stage is dark.*

MARGUERITE:
>April the sixteenth, fifteen hundred and forty-two.
>On that day we sailed from La Rochelle.

>>*The lights go up, revealing the deck of a sailing ship, with a conventionalised harbour backdrop.*

>>*MARGUERITE, ROBERVAL, the GOVERNOR and a few GENTLEMEN stand by the mainmast.*

11

GOVERNOR:

In the name of His Majesty, Francis, King of France,
I give you, Jean de la Roque, Sieur de Roberval,
God-speed upon your expedition. May you annex
wide new domains to His Majesty's crown, may you
populate them in his name with these worthy men
and women, the fine flower of this realm of France,
who travel at your orders. May you gain ample
riches to support our wars at home and establish
the glory of our land and of the true Catholic faith
as beacons in the darkest corners of the earth!

ROBERVAL:

My Lord Governor, on the honour of Jean de la
Roque, I swear that before next winter's snow drift
over the northern lands, I shall have found there a
New France that will shine like a gleaming jewel
in the crown of his most Catholic Majesty.

*The churchbells sound. There is cheering
and shouting. Then the light fades except for
that which shines on ROBERVAL and
MARGUERITE. The sounds of wind and
creaking timbers suggest the movement of
the ship.*

ROBERVAL:

The sails puff out like canvas breasts of giants.
The wind grinds in the spars like freedom.
France falls away from sight within the past
Like headlands dropping into mist.
Far in the west our new home waits untrodden
And there our kindred's constellation rises
And yours, within it, gleams, my niece.
Are you content?

MARGUERITE:

I am content to be with you, my uncle, yet . . .

ROBERVAL:

Yet? Doubts on a day like this?

12

MARGUERITE:
> A little fear, sir.

ROBERVAL:
> Fear? What do you fear? New lands?
> Strange races fierce like painted devils?
> Wild seas like mountains topped with crags of ice?
> I had such fears. Far off, things grow in size.
> The mind reverses all the eye's perspectives,
> And the unknown is monstrous to the untravelled.
> It rears gigantic shapes against the distance
> And shrinks within the telescope of knowledge.
> For men are men and lands are lands world over,
> And waiting for the bold. What do you fear?

MARGUERITE:
> Not the far lands or the strange races, sir.
> It is . . . this fine flower of the realm of France . . .
> Who sail around us.

ROBERVAL:
> Fine flower! Thieves, drabs and parricides
> Wished on me in the place of honest farmers!
> To do me honour all the jails were emptied
> And rogues swim in my forecastles like grey vermin.
> I will break their wills
> And bend their devious natures to my pride.
> Each sprig of treason I will snap off sharp,
> And if one man upon your beauty leers
> He'll feel an iron hand.

MARGUERITE:
> Soften your iron with mercy, uncle.

ROBERVAL:
> Soften! With mercy? So you preach,
> Beg mercy like a friar! Your fear
> Seems blinded by a feeling for what's feared.
> There's no man on this ship whose blood is proud
> And pure like ours. Remember that.

MARGUERITE:
>My pride is what I am, sir.

ROBERVAL:
>Woman's pride weakens with the moon and tide.
>But see that yours stays firm!

>*He exits.*

MARGUERITE:
>Pride! Honour! Blood and bombast!
>The clattering words of empty family legends!
>That is not life, and I must live. Marie!

>*MARIE enters.*

MARIE:
>My lady?

MARGUERITE:
>Did you see him? Did he come to the quay?

MARIE:
>He was not on the quay, my lady.

MARGUERITE:
>He did not even think me worth a message?

MARIE:
>I saw him, my lady, but not upon the quay.

>*She whispers importantly.*

>He's here!

MARGUERITE:
>Here? On the ship?

MARIE:
>On this ship, my lady. He listed as an *arquebusier*.

MARGUERITE:
>   Michel is here!

MARIE:
>   Here — waiting to see you.

MARGUERITE:
>   Bring him . . . no . . . not here, Marie!
>   My uncle would kill him if he found him here.

MARIE:
>   I'll find a place, my lady.

The light fades.

Scene Three

The setting is a cabin on the ship.

MICHEL:
>   Time lies before us. All our life's stretched out
>   In an unending cord. We'll tell it in our hands
>   Each hour a bead in love's bright rosary.

MARGUERITE:
>   It cannot be, Michel. We'll always love like this,
>   In secret, trapped in masks of fear.

MICHEL:
>   It can be, and it will.

MARGUERITE:
>   How can it ever be?
>   We live as prisoners on my uncle's ship.

MICHEL:
>
> But once the sea is crossed and on that shore
> Of ultimate wilderness we set our feet,
> Then we'll be free.

MARGUERITE:
>
> He'll rule there too
> As fiercely as he rules upon his ships.
> Just as the sea makes walls of crystal here
> So will the forest raise its green walls there.
> We'll not be free, never, until our deaths.
> Words here and there, a glance across a room,
> Scarce, furtive meetings at the servants' mercy.
> Anxiety, perhaps a little blackmail . . .
> That will be our love, our rosary of darkness
> Told out till you lose patience and forget me
> Or I hide in a convent's darkness to avoid
> The foul disease of an unwelcome marriage.

MICHEL:
>
> So young, so solemn, so resigned to fate!
> Learn hope! Trust your Michel! I'll find the way
> To tame the wilderness and make it ours.
> Into the woods we'll run and there we'll live
> The poem of our love while hatred dies.

MARGUERITE:
>
> Michel, you talk in fancies like a poet
> Pleasing the ladies out in Fontainebleau.
> There'll be no shepherds in the lands we find
> To play their lovesongs on the pipes of straw,
> But Indians roving through the woods for prey.
> I know you're proud and brave, but can you halt
> A thousand warriors with one arquebus?

MICHEL:
>
> A thousand warriors can be our friends.
> Those green walls will protect and not confine.
> Listen to my secret!

MARGUERITE:

 A secret kept from me?

MICHEL:

 A secret kept from you! Hear it. Ten years ago
 Jacques Cartier brought an Indian chief to France.
 A few sad months he strutted round the court,
 Tricked out in ruffles, a parody of kingship,
 With all his savage dignity turned clownish.
 I helped him once, and then he gave me this . . .

MARGUERITE:

 What is it? Let me hold it. A strange bird,
 Stiff, crude and heavy in the hand,
 And yet so full of life it wants to fly.
 What is it?

MICHEL:

 Some magic image — I hardly followed him.
 He said I'd be their brother if I showed it,
 Free in their forests and their friendship.
 And there's our passport to the wilderness.

MARGUERITE:

 Give me the bird again. The bird of hope.
 A falcon high to fly as our love flies.
 But till we reach the land, be careful.
 My uncle too has bird's blood in his heart.
 His bird's the raven. His brain is cunning,
 His eye is clear, his beak is sharp,
 And we are at his mercy.

MICHEL:

 I'll be as wily as the wisest fox
 And trick him of his booty.

MARGUERITE:

 I am no man's booty.
 I give myself, Michel. I am not taken.
 Go, and trust no one. The ship is full of envy.

MICHEL: *laughing*
Like the world!

The light fades.

Scene Four

The setting is the ship's deck.

LEVEQUE:
There's land, my lord! The watch has just cried out.

ROBERVAL:
The land! Where?

LEVEQUE:
Look to the north, my lord.

ROBERVAL:
A mist-white shore, black forest, endless sky!
And out beyond, where our eyes cannot see,
Where only eagles see, the land unknown,
League beyond league, unknown to Christian men!
This is the kingdom of our hope, pathless and empty.
Its game shall feed us, gold shall glut us, its deep soil
Our sons shall marry and make rich with seeding.
Double the watch. Call the first sight of man —
A boat, a hovel, smoke above the trees.
We'll run ashore, start trade and find a guide
To lead us to the kingdoms of the river.

LEVEQUE:
It was a bad thing Master Cartier
Would not turn back with us, my lord!
He knows the river of St. Lawrence
As no man on our ships does.

ROBERVAL:
>Would not turn back? Dared not! He ran away,
>Stealing into the foggy night from Newfoundland.
>But my revenge will catch him up in France.
>I'll tolerate no traitors. And my mind
>Is not at ease today. My crew — those jailbirds —
>Have kept too silent. Not a growl of anger!
>And dogs should growl cooped up in seaboard kennels.
>What have you heard?

LEVEQUE:
>The crew is quiet, sir.

ROBERVAL:
>And . . . ? What else is in your mind?

LEVEQUE:
>Only one thing, my lord,
>And that may well mean nothing.

ROBERVAL:
>I will judge that, Leveque.

LEVEQUE:
>Then, sir, your niece . . .

ROBERVAL:
>Yes?

LEVEQUE:
>. . . is meeting young Sansterre.

ROBERVAL:
>Sansterre! Leveque,
>Be careful how you speak about my kin.

LEVEQUE:
>You shall judge, as you said, sir. My servant
Courted Marie, the servant of your niece,
And found the girl disdainful.
One day he saw her whispering with Sansterre,
Grew jealous, followed the young gentleman,
And found him meeting not the maid Marie
But Madame Marguerite. Full with the news
He brought his story straight to me,
And I with gold staunched his garrulity
And kept the tale for you.

ROBERVAL:
>As I suspected — servants' gossip.
The empty chatter of men too long at sea
Whose minds run thick with boredom!
Bring no more idle tales against my blood
Or I will splash in yours! Go!

LEVEQUE:
>My lord!

>*He exits.*

ROBERVAL:
>Sansterre! A common *arquebusier*,
Son of a broken squire,
Landless, moneyless, sinking into the people!
I remember him! A smiling, shabby brat,
Standing in the corner of the hall,
Dining at the bottom of the table,
Silent, forgotten, nameless!
But nameless men we do not see or hear,
They pass us in the street like voiceless shadows,
And always it is danger unperceived,
The peril without voice, that harms us most,
Striking our lives below the guard of reason.
Love is beyond reason also. She may love him,
And now I fear she does. Women are devious.
Do I give in to fear?
Let landless breeds be mingled with my blood

20

And steal from me what's mine? No nameless stallion
Shall plough the meadow of my kindred! Leveque!

LEVEQUE enters.

LEVEQUE:
    My lord, you call me?

ROBERVAL:
    I spoke in haste, Leveque.
    That my good niece consorts with young Sansterre
    I doubt. Once as a child she knew him.
    What is more natural than that former playmates
    Should meet upon a ship and talk together?

LEVEQUE:
    Nothing more natural, my lord.

ROBERVAL:
    My niece is blameless.

LEVEQUE:
    It is imprinted on my heart, sir.

ROBERVAL:
    Let it stay there. But I suspect Sansterre
    On other grounds. These younger sons
    Of younger sons — ambition is their food
    And strife's their drink for lack of better nurture.
    They seek to remake fortune without thought
    Of loyalty or honour. They are the cancers
    Swollen with envy whence betrayal spreads.
    Quiz him, Leveque. Question him, lead him on,
    Trip him when he is flattered. You know the game.

LEVEQUE:
    I know the game, my lord.

Scene Five

*The scene takes place in a cabin. MICHEL and
LEVEQUE are drinking at a table.*

MICHEL:
> If I were master of this fleet now,
> I would win glory for us all, Leveque.
> Great Cortez was a poor man like myself.
> He trailed behind the swords of other men
> And then his fortune was a sun of gold
> And empires fell before him.

LEVEQUE:
> Breeding and blood — the only things that count!
> And you . . .

> *He laughs ambiguously.*

> . . . you have them both, Master Sansterre!

MICHEL:
> De Sansterre!

LEVEQUE: *cringing ironically*
> De Sansterre! Forgive me, sir! More wine?
> Don't spare the flask! That democratic jerkin
> Makes me forget your rank. To blood and breeding!

> *They clink glasses and laugh together.*

> Now, Monsieur de Sansterre, if you were General . . .
> Just for the sake of argument . . . if you were General,
> How would you treat the Indians of the river?

MICHEL: *speaking with tipsy solemnity*
> To deal with Indians you need to know them.

LEVEQUE:
> A dazzling thought, sir!

MICHEL:
> You need to know their minds! Their hearts!
> How they must think and how they feel!

LEVEQUE: *laughing*
> And how they love their wives? But neither you
> Nor I know these things.

MICHEL:
> I knew an Indian once.

LEVEQUE:
> Indeed?

MICHEL: *ponderously*
> I studied him
> Hour after hour, and noted how his thoughts
> Fitted together in their Indian pattern
> Like snowflakes making snow.

LEVEQUE:
> Like snowflakes making snow!
> Let us drink to the image! Like snowflakes making snow!
> Blood can make poets then, as well as generals!
> But let us pause a moment, young Cortez.
> I thought you had never crossed the seas before.

MICHEL:
> This is my first voyage, as I told you.

LEVEQUE:
> How did you meet your Indian? In a dream?

MICHEL:
> He was the chief whom Cartier brought to France.

LEVEQUE:
> That was the man! Well, I am sure you charmed him!
> You have a way with you, Monsieur de Sansterre.
> Men are open with you. They show their hearts . . .
> And you show yours in turn!

He laughs, almost insolently.

MICHEL:
    But hearts say more than tongues.
    And with that Indian chief there was a flash
    That leapt across our strangeness, heart to heart.
    Look at this, Leveque! He gave it to me
    Before he died.

LEVEQUE:
    A bird of stone!

    He laughs.

    It won't fly far, my friend!

MICHEL:
    The Indian said it was a hawk — a talisman,
    An emblem of his gods. He said that if I showed it
    The Indians would take me as their brother . . .

LEVEQUE:
    Then your sun of gold has risen.
    You have the key to fortune and to power. . . .
    There is no limit with the Indians' friendship!
    Here's to your future! Boy! Another flask!

    The light fades upon their laughter.

Scene Six

The setting is ROBERVAL's cabin.

ROBERVAL sits at a table, LEVEQUE standing beside him.

ROBERVAL:
    The case is clear — a case of treason!

MICHEL:
>I have committed no treason, sir.
>I have done nothing that might harm the king.

ROBERVAL:
>Treason is in the thought before the doing.
>The heart betrays. The hand is but the tool.
>You have done nothing, but your bad intention
>Starved of success is an intention still.
>Your plans were treason, though they went astray.
>That is enough for death.

MICHEL:
>I neither thought nor acted treason, sir.

ROBERVAL:
>The signs do not support you.

>*There is an urgent knocking.*

>Send them away, Leveque.

MARGUERITE: *calling from within*
>Let me in, Master Leveque! I must speak to my uncle!

LEVEQUE:
>No, Madame, No!

MARGUERITE:
>I will come in! Don't try to stop me!

LEVEQUE:
>Nobody can come in, my lady.

ROBERVAL:
>Let her come in, Leveque, and look at treason.

>*MARGUERITE enters.*

>Let her see how men who eat our bread
>Become our enemies.

MARGUERITE:
>Michel an enemy! It is not true!

ROBERVAL:
>Sit and listen, child, and you shall hear.
>You will admit, Monsieur de Sansterre, that in France
>You gained the friendship of the Indian chief,
>And that he gave you this strange pagan image,
>A thing of horror to a Christian eye,
>By showing which his tribe would make you brother.

MICHEL:
>That is the truth, my lord.

ROBERVAL:
>And yet, with this great power in your hand
>You did not, like a true and loyal subject,
>Reveal it to me for the French advantage.
>Instead, you kept it secret for yourself.
>Tell me, Monsieur de Sansterre, did you mean
>To show this image when you met the Indians?

MICHEL:
>I did, sir.

ROBERVAL:
>You meant, then, to make friends in secret
>With savages, the enemies of France,
>Dead souls outside salvation.
>I must assume you meant to plot against me.
>Why else this secrecy? What else but treason?

MICHEL:
>I meant no treason.

ROBERVAL:
>You had another motive?

MICHEL:
>I had, sir.

ROBERVAL:
>Name it.

MICHEL:
>I cannot.

ROBERVAL: *laughing*
>You cannot! Of course!

MICHEL:
>I will not, then.

MARGUERITE:
>But I can . . . and I will!

ROBERVAL:
>You? My niece! What do you know of this?

MARGUERITE:
>Yes, I! Your niece! This gentleman and I,
>To wed in peace, away from tyranny,
>Made up our minds to reach the Indians' land
>And join their brotherhood among the forests.
>I gave my full consent to him in secret
>And now I give it openly.

ROBERVAL:
>You give your consent? To this landless man,
>This hungry squire's son trailing his musket,
>You give your consent! You, a la Roque!
>You have no consent to give, my niece.
>I am your family. Your fate lies in my hand.
>I will not give you to the poor and mean.

MARGUERITE:
>I give myself! I love for love, not pride!

LEVEQUE:
>There's pride in what she says, my lord. Take care!

ROBERVAL:
>Silence, Leveque! When prides clash, mine will win.
>Now this man's treachery has a double face —
>To join the foe and steal the viceroy's niece!
>Such double crimes can only lead to death.
>You die today, Sansterre.

MARGUERITE:
>You shall not have him!

ROBERVAL:
>You have not right to him. You are not his wife.

MARGUERITE:
>I bear his child.

ROBERVAL: *exclaiming in shocked astonishment*
>you bear his child!

MICHEL: *shouting*
>It's not true, my lord!

ROBERVAL:
>She lies like a madwoman! Put her out, Leveque!

MARGUERITE:
>I have told the truth.

ROBERVAL:
>If that's the truth, it's the worst crime of all.
>The man who stains my kindred shall not live
>To boast his triumph.

MARGUERITE:
>Then I will not live. I'll die if you kill him.

ROBERVAL:
>Die? Of sorrow perhaps? No one dies of sorrow.
>God sends it as a lingering punishment.

MARGUERITE:
> I will kill myself.

ROBERVAL:
> I'll have you well watched over.

MARGUERITE:
> Death wears a thousand masks.
> You cannot penetrate them all, sir.
> I'll find a way to die, and when I go
> My child goes with me. Three deaths on your soul
> And two of your own kin!

ROBERVAL: *aside*
> Two of my kin! That's something for remorse!
> I cannot fix the cord on that fair neck
> And live in peace.

> *He speaks aloud.*

> Banishment, then, not death!
> Niece, this man lives, if you will go with him
> Into the exile I shall choose.

MARGUERITE:
> My only joy shall be to follow him.

ROBERVAL:
> And you will buy your life at such a price?

MICHEL:
> I shall buy more than life, sir.

ROBERVAL:
> Let it be, then.
> What is that island to the south, Leveque?

LEVEQUE:
> It is called the Island of Demons, my lord.
> An Indian tale. They say the demons live there.

ROBERVAL:
Do you believe in demons, niece?

MARGUERITE:
I have not met a man who saw one.

ROBERVAL:
So disbelief you pile on disobedience.
Now you shall try the question for yourself.
You and your lover planned to run away
Into the green shades of the wilderness.
There is your wilderness — that demon's island.
You shall have all you need . . . your servant,
Axes and spades, the tools to build a hut,
Food of the flesh you shall not want,
But in the spirit you may starve.
No priest will ever join your hands,
No holy baptist give your child a name,
No blessed voices sing your orisons
When you are laid within the alien earth.
And if no visible demons rend your peace,
Do not forget the demon named Regret.
There is the sentence. Do you still accept?

MICHEL AND
MARGUERITE:
We do.

ROBERVAL:
Ferry them over to their paradise,
Far from the path where I sail on alone
To claim my glory and my destiny.

Scene Seven

The stage is dark.

*The sounds of water lapping against a boat
and our dipping into a calm sea are heard.*

MARGUERITE:
There was the great beach, and brown ropes of kelp
Knotted in the rocks, and the shattered trees
Piled in a bulwark where the storms had stamped,
And the forest stood in a palisade behind them
Hiding our future in its darkness.
Over the beach and in the forest
Nothing stirred but birds whirling in the sky
And birds floating in white fleets on the water
And birds crying from the rockpools with plaintive piping.
And in my hand the bird of stone
Nestled like a token of Eden.
On the damp sand the sailors unloaded the stores.
I stood on the edge of the wood and smelt the season
And saw the pale wild roses gleam in the shadow.
I plucked them, and wept as I heard the oars splash
And watched the sailors go. We were alone.
I wept for joy, not sorrow.

Scene Eight

*The scene is set on the island, with a backdrop
of beach and forest.*

*Sounds are heard of the surf breaking and the
gulls crying plaintively.*

MARGUERITE:
They are unfurling the sails. The wind fills them
And the ship moves away to the west like a great white
  bird
Forsaking its offspring.

MICHEL:
Not a pennon breaks on the mast.
The ship might be full of blind men as it sails
Trailing into the distance all the cords of our past.

MARGUERITE:
>Those cords are broken. We are exiles now
>And exiles have only the future. God takes away the rest
>And gives us a new beginning.

MICHEL:
>We dreamt of it night and day! A new beginning!
>An island where the wild vine grows like love
>Tangling in freedom from the frosts of hate.

MARGUERITE:
>Why do you weep, Marie, when we are laughing?

MARIE:
>You laugh for your new beginning.
>I weep for the past and a bitter ending.
>I weep for my home and the voices I loved.

MARGUERITE:
>We will make a new home, better than you remember.

MICHEL:
>I will take our axes and carve from the forest
>A fair domain without lord or lackey
>And down the dark woods we will hunt like angels
>And rule over the beasts like Adam in Eden.

MARIE:
>Adam was innocent in Eden's garden.
>I weep for innocence never returning.

MARGUERITE:
>But here on this island all guilt shall vanish
>Away from gold and the world's temptation.

MICHEL:
>And we shall be innocent under the sun
>Like animals bright in their natural light.

MARIE:
>I am a servant. My father tills the soil
>On the barrenest headland of Brittany.
>I cannot talk with you, and yet I know
>We go not back to Eden, and we go
>Forward to Heaven only by the word
>I cannot read, and by the cross,
>And the spirit hovering dovelike over
>The thorned and bleeding head.

MARGUERITE:
>We too are led by love and a spirit.
>The spirit of freedom! Here is its bird.
>The falcon soars above the passive dove.

MARIE:
>My lady, you hold in your hand a piece of stone.

MICHEL:
>It is a stone filled with the faith of men
>Who have learnt to live in the wilderness.

MARIE:
>It is a stone filled with the sorcery of savages.
>If you had not owned it we should not be cast
>On this Island of Demons.

MARGUERITE:
>If we had not owned it
>We should not be free to live, but still be slaves
>Sailing under the tyranny of my uncle's pride.

MARIE:
>And now, my lady, you are ruled by your own pride,
>And by your unblessed love which for my sins
>I fostered as the busy go-between.
>My punishment begins. But I am only a servant.
>I say too much. I will go to gather wood
>And make a fire and start the daily life.

>*She exits.*

MARGUERITE:
>	She talked of pride. She said — "Your unblessed love."
>	Do you believe our love can be unblessed?

MICHEL:
>	Blessing's a word without the thing that's blessed,
>	And no priest's mumbling makes a love more true.
>	All lies within ourselves — evil and good —
>	And we can make this island blessed Eden . . .

MARGUERITE:
>	And we can make it Hell. The logic follows.

MICHEL:
>	But we shall not, for Hell's not in our love.
>	Look — the green forest opens to the headland
>	And calls us to explore. The sky is dark with birds.
>	We'll take our guns, and start upon our way
>	To claim the island.

>	*They leave, and the three DEMONS enter,
>	looking after them and laughing. The
>	DEMONS are dressed in the style of modern
>	public relations men.*

1ST DEMON:
>	And so they run like children up the shore,
>	Laughing, all sadness gone, not in the least aware
>	That now it's all beginning, not aware
>	Even of my presence. But that in itself
>	Is not surprising, since it takes some time
>	For the mind to acclimatize itself to *us*.
>	By *us* I mean the Demons. Yes, I am the Demon of
>	 Doubt.
>	Let me say now, right at the beginning
>	That I have no connection with the Island's name.
>	The link is an impure coincidence. Any island
>	Is an Island of Demons, and any mind, for that matter.
>	We are not always active. Long we lie latent;
>	A moment's impulse calls us back to life;
>	The gates creak open, we dash into the fortress,

We become, to use the jargon, activated.
A moment ago, for instance, I was not present,
Sitting in my shred of intangibility,
And now I am, and yet I did not travel,
Nor, in the strict sense, was I born at that moment.
I was, as it were, plucked out of nothing
As a note is plucked through an instrument.
I vibrated to life in that sharp second
When the maid's words struck home in Marguerite,
And doubt — which is myself — rose in her mind.
I did not rise along. Let me introduce my brethren.

2ND DEMON:
My name is Discord.

3RD DEMON:
My name is Regret.

1ST DEMON:
Doubt, Discord, Regret — thought, action, consequence!
We always work together, a trinity of negation.
Sometimes we work on our own, but now we have an ally.

A wolf howl is heard offstage.

Quite inarticulate, you'll observe. An animal sound!
It is the spirit of the island — not a demon,
For only human souls give the rich food
That demons feed on, but a firm ally,
For, like the beasts, Nature distrusts Man's smell,
And works for his destruction. Now I'll withdraw.
You'll see our hands in turn behind the action.

The light fades on the scene.

Scene Nine

The scene is set outside a log hut. MARGUERITE and MARIE are plucking wild duck.

A shot sounds from the distance.

MARGUERITE:
>Today he's hunting along this shore.
>Always hunting! As if some hungry hand
>Twisted his heart and drove him to destroy.

MARIE:
>We have to eat. He keeps us well supplied.

MARGUERITE:
>He does not kill to keep us well supplied.
>He kills because he has the hunter's lust;
>A dog gone wild will turn upon the sheep.
>Life stirs in me, and death strikes from his hand,
>And innocent birds fall from the sky and rot
>Because he is restless!

MARIE:
>Gentlemen like to hunt.

MARGUERITE:
>This is no place for gentlemen. There are things
>That need making, things for the hand to do,
>And he disdains to touch his hands with toil.

MARIE:
>It will pass, my lady. He's restless, as you say.

MARGUERITE:
>He's coming now. There! Over the rocks,
>Another dead beast hunched across his shoulders.

MICHEL: *shouting offstage*
Marguerite!

He enters, a dead buck on his shoulder.

Look! Five points to his antlers!

MARGUERITE:
Five points to the mighty Nimrod!

MICHEL:
Aren't you glad? More food for the smokehouse!

MARGUERITE:
We've all we need. Let the beasts live.
You kill too many. One day we shall starve.

MICHEL:
Not on this island! The woods run thick with game
Like rivers filled with salmon in the spring.

MARGUERITE:
You never finished thatching the shed roof.
Stay here, Michel, and get it done tomorrow.

MICHEL:
The shed roof? Perhaps I will. I'll need some reeds.
I saw three wolves at noon, and by the marsh
The spoor of a great bear. One day I'll hunt him.

MARGUERITE:
What use is a bear to us?

MICHEL:
His skin can keep us warm.

MARGUERITE:
You'd risk your life to steal a poor beast's hide!

MICHEL:

    I'll conquer this island. I'll make the beasts bow down
    So that they'd call me king if they could speak!

MARGUERITE:

    The cradle still needs making. The wood for the fire
    Is heavy for me now. Marie is tired.

MICHEL:

    You talk at me always, as if I were
    Like Hercules, obedient to a woman.
    I'm no man's servant and no woman's!
    I'll do my work, and do it when I will,
    Hunt when I will, and answer to myself.

MARGUERITE:

    That wasn't what you said the day we came here.
    That is a long time ago. We have all changed now.

MICHEL:

    No . . . that isn't what I said. I haven't changed,
    And yet some days it seems a demon whispers. . . .

MARGUERITE:

    All is in your mind!

MICHEL:

    Of course! I don't believe in demons.
    Don't worry. I will stay, finish the roof,
    Build the cradle, dig the ground for seed.
    Give me that stick there — and my knife.

MARGUERITE:

    Your hunting tally?

MICHEL:

    No — the tally of days. There — two hundred and
        twenty-one!
    Two hundred and twenty-one days! More than seven
        months!

MARGUERITE:
Soon it will be spring.

MICHEL:
There were green buds down by the marsh
Where the snows melt first. Another year
Well on its way to Heaven.

MARGUERITE:
And you regret it.
You regret all the days we have spent on this island.

MICHEL:
Regret! What puts it in your mind that I regret?

MARGUERITE:
I see you cut each day deep with your knife
As if you cut a fragment from your heart.

MICHEL:
Your thoughts run wild. I haven't known
More happiness in all my life than this —
Freedom — with you! Forget your doubts!

MARGUERITE: *bitterly*
That's what I would like!
To forget my doubts!

MICHEL: *speaking after a brief silence*
Where is Marie?

MARGUERITE:
She must have gone down to the beach again.

MICHEL:
>The beach! Yes, she'll be there! Look — that's her smoke!
>She cannot gather firewood for the hut,
>But every day, in rainfall and in sun,
>She goes down to the beach and lights her fire,
>And watches the blue flames licking out the salt
>Along the driftwood, and gazes at the smoke
>As if an angel would flash out, and then she looks
>Out to the sea with damp and longing eyes.

MARGUERITE:
>She sits as Breton women always sit
>Waiting for sails across the white horizon
>That brings their men back from the fishing banks.
>Their life is half spent watching out for sails.

MICHEL:
>She has no fisher husband, but she longs
>To leave the island and to go from us.
>Some days I see that fire and burn with rage
>As kings must burn when they see traitors' plans.
>I'll go and beat it out before her eyes!

MARGUERITE:
>Leave her alone, Michel! She does no harm.
>The fire is all she has. Its flames
>Construct the shape of everything she loves
>Framed in the fragile hope the smoke sends up.

MICHEL:
>And if some ship comes answering to her signal?

MARGUERITE:
>No ship will come, and if one does, she'll stay
>If we decide to stay.

MICHEL:
>If we decide to stay!
>You speak as if you doubt it.

MARGUERITE:
> No, but your anger makes me think you may.

MICHEL:
> You've said too much. I'll stay to hear no more.
> I'll take my gun and go the path I must
> To fight the island and to win myself . . .

MARGUERITE:
> It will be dark soon. In an hour we eat.

MICHEL:
> Eat by yourself, and leave the dark to me.
> I'll walk upon this island how I will
> And when, and where. . . .

MARGUERITE:
> Go, then! Go! I cannot stand your talk!

> *He goes out, slamming the door.*

> Go! Let him go!

> *She breaks into sobbing.*

> *A wolf howl is heard in the distance, as the light fades on the scene.*

Scene Ten

> *The scene is set inside the cabin where MARIE and MARGUERITE are waiting in rough, handhewn chairs.*

> *A rush light burns.*

MARGUERITE:
> Make up the fire, Marie. It's getting colder.

MARIE:

>There's more ice coming down upon the beaches.
>I heard it pile and crackle in the night.

MARGUERITE:

>It's getting light outside.

>>*The howl of a wolf is heard again, this time
>>nearer the cabin.*

>The beast again!

MARIE:

>They always come when ice is on the shore.

MARGUERITE:

>And every time my heart leaps with foreboding.

MARIE:

>We're safe here, in the hut.

MARGUERITE:

>But Michel isn't here.

MARIE:

>He has his gun. We've heard no shooting.
>Where do you think he went, my lady?

MARGUERITE:

>You know as well as I do where he went.
>He went to find the bear spoor in the marsh.
>To find the island and to win himself!
>That was what he said, and in my pride
>I shouted to him "Go!" and let him go!
>I should have thrown myself upon the ground
>And howled and begged and clung around his feet,
>I should . . .

MARIE:

> There's nothing you could do, my lady.
> When a man wants to go he goes, whether he comes
> Back with the sun or not. My father went,
> My brother too, and they did not come back.
> They had to go, and we could only hope
> And tell our beads, and wait the fleet's return.

MARGUERITE:

> You think Michel will not come back.

MARIE:

> I did not say it. He is in God's hands.

MARGUERITE:

> Or in the Devil's.

MARIE:

> Our prayers can keep the Devil off.

MARGUERITE:

> Our prayers! You pray for both! I'll find Michel.
> It's light now. Give me my cloak, and the spare gun.

MARIE:

> Where are you going, my lady? Remember your child!

MARGUERITE:

> The unborn child? First native of the island!

> *She laughs bitterly.*

> He'll take his chance with me, and you can pray.
> I'll trust to my own hand.

> *A shot is heard in the distance*

> It's from the marsh!

MARIE:

> I'll go with you.

MARGUERITE:
> Come then! There's no time! I know there is no time!

> *They go out.*

> *The light fades, but a moment later the spotlight illuminates the 1ST DEMON, in the centre of the stage.*

1ST DEMON:
> So I appear again. Now, like a Greek chorus
> To keep the theatre tidy and describe
> The dread deeds off the stage. O, I admit
> I feel the horror too. We demons
> Are more human than you think. After all,
> You breed us in your hearts.
> Besides, being the Demon of Doubt,
> I naturally doubt myself and all my schemes,
> And even my demoniac heart was troubled
> To float invisible and see it all,
> The clawed-up body grasping its broken gun
> Among the shattered flower buds where the water
> Sogged upward through the grass at every step.
> The women came, and wept as women must,
> And dragged the body on to the dry land,
> Where the maid carried rocks and piled them high
> To keep the beasts away. And made a cross
> To keep us away. That night the child was born.
> It did not live. Our schemes were working out.
> Discord and Doubt — we'd played our parts.
> The rest was yet to come.

Scene Eleven

The women are inside the cabin.

It is daylight.

MARGUERITE:
> He came because of me. Whatever you say, Marie,
> Except for me he would not have joined the ship.
> He would have been alive at home, perhaps
> Loving another girl and marrying,
> Getting a little sinecure . . . and living. . . .

MARIE:
> There was nothing you could do, my lady.
> He loved you and he came. You were not to blame.
> You were not to blame either for your uncle's anger,
> And if you had not come to the island with him,
> Michel would have died on the rope. His time had come.

MARGUERITE:
> It is so easy to blame fate for our own errors.
> However you may say it, he met his death
> From knowing me.

MARIE:
> He met his death from the Evil One!

MARGUERITE:
> You still chatter of evil spirits. I believe
> In what I touch and see and feel within me.
> What I feel is the remorse that eats my heart
> With the knowledge that without me he might live.

MARIE:
> He died from sorcery.

MARGUERITE:

    Sorcery and demons!
    Your everlasting masks to hide the truth!
    If anyone bewitched him, it was I.
    I made no doll of wax, I burnt no fire
    Of magic leaves, and yet I took his heart. . . .

MARIE:

    He trusted fortune to a graven image.

MARGUERITE:

    The bird of stone! It was a talisman.

MARIE:

    He thought it would work wonders. You did also.
    Have you forgotten your own words, my lady?

MARGUERITE:

    I have not. I believed in it. I believed
    A thing of stone had some mysterious impulse
    To raise our fortunes like a tropic vine
    Upon this chilly shore. It was a symbol
    And nothing more.

MARIE:

    It was the Devil's sign.

MARGUERITE:

    I know no devils and I know no angels.
    It was a sign pointing to nothing. A stone
    With meaning only for the men who made it.
    Now, to please you, I'll throw it in the fire.

MARIE:

    It lies in the red cavern of embers
    Like a black salamander. It is cracking apart!
    The image has broken!

MARGUERITE:

> As you say, the image has broken.
> Something has gone from my mind, and in its place
> There is only grief and a faceless anguish.

MARIE:

> There could be faith, my lady.

MARGUERITE:

> Faith is a gift, and when it is not given
> One's life becomes a tunnel where the soul
> Waits vainly for an ear to hear its guilt,
> Throbs like the pulse of a decaying heart
> And asks consoling answers. I killed Michel!
> I killed my child! I know my guilt.

MARIE:

> You are innocent of both, my lady.

MARGUERITE:

> No one is innocent. At best the case is unproven.
> But I'm as guilty of that double death
> As if fate's claws were grafted on my fingers.
> I was the accomplice of their destiny
> When I agreed to seek our joy in flight.
> Better a lifetime as my uncle's prisoner
> Than the grim joys that liberty has brought!

> *She laughs nervously.*

> Well, we have come to an ending, Marie,
> And every ending means a new beginning.
> How do *we* begin? Two solitary women
> Trapped on an island where the spring comes slowly
> And men are extinct, and the wolves howl at the door.
> We'll live, of course. I can shoot birds, and fish,
> And hunt, as Michel did. We'll make our fire
> Each morning on the beach, and if a ship
> Comes we'll go home, if home seems worth it then.
> But what will be the sense and what the savour
> Of each day dawning in the endless cycle

With no magnetic goal to give it meaning,
No love, no child, no future, no peace . . .

*The 3RD DEMON enters and stands in a
corner.*

3RD DEMON:

No peace, of course, there is no peace for you.
But do not think you can escape the future.
Memory will walk like a ghost those endless days,
And I shall be there too, always beside you.
You will ever be lonely, never be alone.

MARGUERITE:

What did you say? Who are you?

3RD DEMON:

I am Regret. You called me from the void.

MARGUERITE:

Regret!

MARIE:

My lady! What is it? What are you saying?

MARGUERITE:

It was strange. I heard a voice
As if there were someone whispering in the corner.
It has stopped now, and there is no one there.

MARIE:

I heard nothing.

MARGUERITE:

It was a voice for me only.
It was my nerves, my imagination. . . .

MARIE:

Perhaps it was an angel.

MARGUERITE:

No angel spoke like that.

MARIE:

Then it was a demon. The demons speak in voices
Imitating the voices of the angels.
When I was young a girl I knew heard voices.

MARGUERITE:

What did they tell her?

MARIE:

They destroyed her. She burnt.

MARGUERITE:

In Hell?

MARIE:

In the square of St. Brieuc.

MARGUERITE:

I'm safe from that. We have no priests among us.

MARIE:

I wish we had.

MARGUERITE:

For burning?

MARIE:

For saving. Have you forgotten what your uncle said
That terrible day he cast you on this island?

MARGUERITE:

What my uncle said? Yes . . . yes . . . I had forgotten. . . .

3RD DEMON:
>Food of the flesh you will not want,
>But in the spirit you may starve.
>No priest will ever join your hands,
>No holy Baptist give your child a name,
>No blessed voices sing your orisons
>When you are laid within that alien earth.
>And if no visible demons rend your peace,
>Do not forget the demon named Regret. . . .

MARGUERITE:
>I wanted to forget, but now it all comes back
>Shouldering into my memory like the man himself.
>That empty boaster spoke the truth, Marie!
>We thought the wilderness would be an Eden.
>If it's an Eden, then the Fall came first.
>Lend me your cross, Marie. The bird of stone
>Is dead. Perhaps another emblem comes to life.

>*The light fades on the scene.*

Scene Twelve

>*A spotlight illuminates the 1ST DEMON in the centre of the stage.*

1ST DEMON:
>We demons thrive best in the subtler minds.
>There are some souls as rocky as the soils
>From which their bodies spring. We find
>Poor foothold in such stony saintliness,
>And these untemptables infect the rest
>With their own stubbornness.
>Take Marie — no talent, no imagination —
>What flightiness she had fled with adversity,
>And left the leathery female pietist.
>Live and let live — we never bear a grudge,
>But her dumb zeal was most insidious,

So, fitting the conclusion to the person,
We crowned her piety with martyrdom.

*Offstage the howling of hunting wolves is heard,
then MARIE's screams, drowned by the yelping
of the pack.*

1ST DEMON:
Need I got into details? Thank you. . . .
I knew you'd think our attitude quite sporting.
Marie went on to her reward in Heaven,
And we prepared the ultimate manoeuvre.

Scene Thirteen

The setting is the beach, with a backdrop of trees.

*MARGUERITE walks up and down. The
DEMONS stand at the back of the stage.*

MARGUERITE:
Another day in the rosary of despair.
It is six months since Marie died, and two years
Since we came to the island, and every day
I walk on the beach and strike my steel on stone
And nurse the sparks to flame until the smoke
Curls and dissolves high in the windy air.
But no ship comes. No answer comes at all.

1ST DEMON:
Do you expect a ship, or any answer?

MARGUERITE:
You here again? So early in the day?

1ST DEMON:
> Yes, here again, faithful and true companion,
> Leaning over your shoulder like a face
> Which the mirror will not reflect. Tell me,
> Since you clearly do not expect a ship,
> Why drag the wood and sear your eyes with smoke?
> Would it not be better to give it up,
> To give it all up, to forget,
> To slide into the snowdrift of surrender
> And sleep that sweet snow sleep of death?

MARGUERITE:
> You always tell me that, and I've no answer
> Except the hand that steals towards the cross
> Here on my waist, and then my heart says no,
> And I must go from daylight into dusk
> And rise again to face the same defeat.

1ST DEMON:
> Your cross is nothing but a shred of tooth
> From some beast's tusk. Throw it into the fire.
> It will burn sooner than the bird of stone.
> What power is in a thing so soon destroyed?

MARGUERITE:
> The power is not the thing. The power is
> A voice that speaks like silence, a remembering
> Of love, and those whose hearts spoke love,
> And that great primal Love. . . .

2ND DEMON:
> One moment please!
> My name is Discord. You have called me often. . . .

MARGUERITE:
> I do not call you now.

2ND DEMON:
> Your words are challenges.
> Those whose hearts spoke love! Do you mean
> Michel? Do you mean Marie?

MARGUERITE:
>I mean them all.

2ND DEMON:
>Did you not quarrel with Michel the night he died?
>Did not Marie run out because you mocked her
>The day the wolves destroyed her? Where was your
>>love then?
>Where was your peace with *them*?

MARGUERITE:
>It is true! It is true!
>I was hateful to them. I drove them from me.

2ND DEMON:
>Hateful, you hated, and for that you are mine!

MARGUERITE:
>Yours! Oh, Marie, help me! No, I'm not yours!
>I hate no longer.

2ND DEMON:
>And your uncle? What about your uncle?
>That tyrannous, boasting, self-righteous hypocrite,
>Who landed your lover on this shore to die,
>And you to follow him. . . . Do you not hate your uncle?

MARGUERITE:
>My uncle! Yes . . . yes . . . I hate . . .

>*The DEMONS snicker triumphantly.*

>No! It is not true! The voice within . . .
>Once I did hate him, but that hate has faded
>Like a burning dawn! I do not feel hate now.

3RD DEMON:
>   You do not hate, you will not doubt,
>   But I have barbs that strike more deep.
>   Don't you recognize my voice? I am Regret.
>   Lady, do you remember the country of your childhood,
>   Those wide French plains swept golden with the wheat
>   Breaking against the grey walls of cathedrals,
>   The wandering streams, the woods, the evening gathering
>   Over the mushroom meadows and the primrose lanes . . .

MARGUERITE:
>   Oh, God, how I remember . . .

3RD DEMON:
>   And do you remember the castle
>   And the arrased rooms, and the chamber in the tower
>   Where you would watch Michel, a poor knight's son,
>   Come riding through the wood to linger shyly
>   In the great hall, almost among the servants.
>   Do you remember?

MARGUERITE: *weeping*
>   Yes . . . yes . . .

3RD DEMON:
>   Yes, you remember. Now do you regret
>   All of that golden past? Do you regret the acts
>   That brought you here, far from that April land,
>   And turned your lover to a feast of carrion?
>   Do you regret them all?

MARGUERITE:
>   Yes, I regret them all. . . .

3RD DEMON:
>   And do you curse the God that made your fate?

MARGUERITE: *replying passionately*
>   No!

3RD DEMON:
>Not quite so vehement, my lady.
>Put it another way. If all those golden days
>Which you regret could be returned to you,
>And all that went between be wiped away,
>Would you curse God to bring it all about?

MARGUERITE:
>Leave me! Leave me in peace!

ALL DEMONS:
>Answer! Answer! Answer!

3RD DEMON:
>Would you curse God? I make you promises.
>No more remorse. And nights as dreamless as an empty
>>slate,
>And all the peace of sweet oblivion. . . .

1ST DEMON:
>You have only to answer.

2ND DEMON:
>Only to curse God. A word is enough.

MARGUERITE:
>No! No! Leave me in peace! Michel! Marie!

>*MARIE enters, transfigured by light.*

1ST DEMON:
>Who is that, standing now beside her?

2ND DEMON:
>In that invisible presence my ardour turns to ice.

>*The light begins to fade on the DEMONS.*

3rd DEMON:
>I feel the snow settle on me. My will ebbs.

MARIE:
>I am Marie, but another Marie also.
>I rise from within you. Your own cries called me forth,
>And in that instant when you denied denial
>You forged your freedom. Demons and protectors
>Alike are bred within the human heart,
>And man in his own will makes under Heaven
>His free way to destruction or to glory.
>Look to the sea.

MARGUERITE:
>The ship sails in from the east like a great white bird
>And all the voices of the island are silent.

Six Dry Cakes for the Hunted

A Canadian Myth

Scene One

ANNOUNCER:

It is the first of June, 1885. An early summer dawn throws long eastward shadows. Its light picks out the stockade of Fort Assiniboine on the American side of the frontier, territory of Montana. It is an empty land, a dead land waiting for a new life. The millions of buffalo, the thousands of their killers, have gone so suddenly that men who do not understand the history they create believe these ghosts from a pristine world will return to fill the solitudes the farmers have not yet populated. The land is alive with rumour. Only two weeks ago, far to the North beside the Saskatchewan River, the rebellion of the Métis against the Canadian government has gone the way of all lost causes. The fort stands alone in its interminable landscape, but this morning the excitement in its courtyard penetrates even the commandant's quarters.

There is a hubbub of voices rising and falling.

COMMANDANT:

Each ordinary morning, I find my boredom on awakening in this Godforsaken post reflected in the movements and faces of the most listless company in the United States Army. Today I look out and see my men chattering around the barracks doors as if for once they had a real interest in existence. Tell me, Lieutenant, what stirs them out of their normal lethargy?

LIEUTENANT:

I came to report, sir. Sergeant Prevost intercepted two horsemen crossing the border. He has arrested them and brought them in.

COMMANDANT:

Arrested them? Do we want them?

LIEUTENANT:

One of them, sir, is Gabriel Dumont!

COMMANDANT:

The Métis! Now that is really interesting. Why should Dumont choose us for his visit?

LIEUTENANT:

A sensible choice, I would say, sir. Well to the west, unpopulated and hilly country to travel through, and a Métis population in our territory.

COMMANDANT:

And I'm told that Dumont knows his way in the prairies like an antelope. Yes, I imagine we should have expected him. Who's his companion?

LIEUTENANT:

One of Riel's councillors.

COMAMANDANT:

Not quite the man I would hope for!

LIEUTENANT:
You'd have preferred Riel, sir?

COMMANDANT: *laughing*
Of course. It would have been a neat turning of
tricks. They gave refuge to Sitting Bull. With Riel on
our hands we'd have evened the score. Fetch them in.

> *Sounds of single footsteps, a brief pause, then
> multiple footsteps on a wooden floor are heard.*

COMMANDANT:
Good morning, gentlemen.

DUMONT:
I am Dumont, Adjutant-General of the Métis nation.

COMMANDANT:
Pleasure to meet a colleague, Monsieur Dumont. And
you, sir?

DUMAS:
Michel Dumas.

COMMANDANT:
May I invite you to breakfast?

DUMAS:
Thank you, Monsieur le Commandant. Your men have
already been hospitable.

COMMANDANT:
I am glad to hear that they have not entirely lost the
social virtues. So, gentlemen, you are here, I assume,
because in your own country you are hunted as
rebels.

DUMONT:

>We are hunted. We have broken no just law, but every trail above the border is alive with horsemen looking for us. Whether that makes us rebels, let your country judge. I am told it is a country that was born in a rebellion. We are only asking for shelter.

COMMANDANT:

>You are not our rebels, Monsieur Dumont. Between us and you there is no quarrel. But I am a subordinate officer. The gift of asylum is not mine. You must understand that. After all, you commanded an army . . .

DUMONT:

>Three hundred hunters, monsieur, fighting from holes, with stones for bullets, until the powder ran out and the priests betrayed us!

COMMANDANT:

>All George Washington led at first was an army of farmers, fighting with old muskets and fowling pieces. Monsieur Dumont, I shall be proud to forward your plea for asylum.

DUMONT:

>Thank you.

COMMANDANT:

>You give your word to stay in the fort until the answer comes?

DUMONT:

>Of course.

COMMANDANT:

>But there is one thing . . .

DUMONT:

>Monsieur?

COMMANDANT:

>It is something that will help me in drafting the telegram. Tell me, why are you on the safe side of the border when your leader is in prison in Regina with his worst enemies guarding the cell?

DUMONT:

>If it had been my will he would have ridden beside me out of the night to give thanks to Our Lady at the border and see the dawn rising over your country.

COMMANDANT:

>I am not impugning your honour, Monsieur Dumont. Your bravery is known throughout the west. Let me put it differently. It would be helpful to my superiors in Washington, who are far away from the frontier, if I could tell them why Louis Riel surrendered to his enemies and you evaded them. Was that his choice? Or was it merely his misfortune and your luck?

DUMONT:

>The answer to that question, Monsieur le Commandant, would need more telling than your patience might accept. I would have to tell you why we fought, what we hoped for, how we were defeated. It would take time, and I have learnt that my people are not important in the eyes of the world. There are a few thousand of us, scattered over the prairies. Our fathers were French, our mothers were Indian. We thought we were both, but in fact we were neither, and our lives were crushed in the gap between. We called ourselves a nation, but the world did not, because the world is not interested in little peoples. Why should you be, Monsieur le Commandant?

COMMANDANT:

>You thought your people important enough to die for if you had to, and to survive for if you could. That is why I would like to hear your story.

DUMONT:

It is a tale like all the tales we tell in the prairies, monsieur. It runs like the sun from season to season, but it never returns to the place where the circle began.

COMMANDANT:

Only men who are lost walk in circles and come back to the point where they started. You have found your way out of the maze, Monsieur Dumont. I would like to follow it with you.

Scene Two

DUMONT:

You might say that it began with the presence of the buffalo, and it ended with the death of the buffalo. Our fathers came to the west from Quebec to collect the skins of little animals to be worn by people we had never seen. But to gain the skins of little animals, the fur traders and their voyageurs had to live in winter in the cold lands of the north, and to sustain them it was necessary to kill the large animals, and especially the buffalo which before memory or even legend began had fed the Indians whose girls became our mothers. It was our misfortune that the wishes of our fathers were not the same as the needs of our mothers, and so we became hunters for the fur traders of Montreal and went into the prairie to kill off the beasts that had sustained our ancestors. Every year we went out from Red River to kill the buffalo and make pemmican. And so the prairie became our home as much as it was the home of the Indians.

DUMAS:

Sometimes twelve hundred carts would go out, with six hundred hunters, all of them Métis, and it became necessary to find a way to prevent conflict among us and yet to assure that every man and every woman and child received what was necessary to live. And so, Monsieur le Commandant, we made our own laws for the buffalo hunt, and since laws need people who carry them out, we turned ourselves each summer into a little travelling nation with its chief who would be a good hunter, and its captains who would keep order and see that nobody broke the rules of the hunt, either by attacking the herd before the word had been given or by failing to provide for those in need. Often it was the family of Dumont from which we chose our chiefs. Gabriel's father Isidore, and his uncle Jean, were both great leaders of the hunt, and Gabriel took after them, though he would not tell you this, and many years ago, after the buffalo had gone from the Red River, and we had to hunt in the western prairies, it was he whom we elected every year as our leader.

DUMONT:

That is an old tale and of no interest now. The buffalo hunt is ended, and who was chief of it has no longer any meaning. What has meaning is that the buffalo are gone, and the Métis are left, and they are men with the needs of men. A long time ago there were some of us who saw that the buffalo could not last for ever, and when this thought came to us the heritage of our French fathers became strong in our minds. We loved to wander, and yet, like bears seeking caves for hibernation, we began to choose places where we could built log shacks to spend the winter, and then we began to plough the land beside the rivers and to buy cattle, and afterwards the priests came among us. Father André founded the mission at St. Laurent, and a little later he built the church of St. Anthony at the place we called Batoche. After what happened at Batoche this year,

I cannot speak of the priests without anger, and yet
God would not forgive me, nor would my conscience,
if I did not say that in those days, when the priests
first came among us, they acted as if they were
indeed fathers who knew the needs of their children.

> *Music — a Métis song — is heard, fading to the
> background voices of a meeting.*

ANDRE:

Men of the Saskatchewan, we are gathered in the eye
of God to create an order that will be pleasing to him.
An order pleasing to God is one in which justice and
mercy meet in a state of equity, in which no man
takes advantage of another, in which the strong
succour the helpless, and in which, recognizing that
by the nature of our condition we are all sinners, a
suitable means is found to discourage crimes that are
harmful to the defenceless and to compensate those
who suffer from them. This is why I have called you
today to the mission of St. Laurent to consider the
need for establishing, here on the open prairie, the
rules of a Christian civil order.

NOLIN:

Father André, there is no one here who will disagree
with what you have said. You speak of what we need.
But I am from the Red River, and I remember that it
is only four years since 1869, when we tried to make
there a Christian order like that you describe. It was
destroyed and Louis Riel who created it was driven
into exile.

ANDRE:

I have not forgotten what happened on the Red River, my son. But our situation is not the same. When Louis Riel took action, he was like a man building a dike against a flood that was already irresistible. Here on the Saskatchewan there is, as yet, nobody who wants our land, nobody who is prepared to govern us. So we should begin to govern ourselves and avoid the fate of your brothers on the Red River.

DUMONT:

I think the good Father talks good sense. All he is telling us is to do what we have done on the prairies every summer since we can remember. Each summer we make our rules for the hunt; they always are the same rules, for a season we obey them, and all of us feel the good of it. Times are changing. Now we are farmers as well as hunters, and perhaps we should think of making our rules last us not only through the summer, but from one Christmas to the next. If they are good for three months, why not for twelve?

There is applause, and shouts of "Bravo, Gabriel!" are heard.

Once we kept our laws in our heads because we could not write. Now that we have the good Father among us, we can get him to write them down for us, and add a few new laws for the times when we are not hunting and therefore more open to temptation.

There is laughter from the assembly.

ANDRE:

>I am willing to act as your secretary and write down your laws. But you must make them yourselves. You must elect those who will administer them. Therefore, I suggest that you choose a president and a council who will work with me to establish the rules of the community of St. Laurent.

DUMAS:

>Gabriel Dumont has never failed us as chief of the hunt. Let him be our president . . .

>*More applause is heard, gradually fading out.*

Scene Three

DUMONT:

>That was in 1873. We established our little government at St. Laurent, and made our laws, and lived by them, and for two years everything went well. We heard that the redcoated police from Canada had come into the prairies, but that was in the south and at first we were not concerned. But very soon we found that there were those who thought they could play the new laws of the Mounted Police against the old law of the prairie. In 1875 the Hudson's Bay Company sent in hunters who defied the laws we had established. I arrested them; one of them I fined. The Company decided to use new law against old law, and told the Mounted Police we were making a rebellion. The Police came to arrest me, but in the end they went away; having decided that I had acted according to the tradition of the prairies, they let me go with a warning. It was a small thing, and yet I was troubled, and I went to Father André with my trouble.

*A church bell tolls monotonously in the back-
ground to the end of this small scene.*

There are enough of us, Father! Give me two years
to buy guns from the Americans, and I can sweep
the redcoats off the prairies!

ANDRE:
The Mounted Police are not buffalo, Gabriel. You
will find them harder to hunt, and even if you do kill
them all, there will be others. And they represent
the law.

DUMONT:
Their law is not ours. Our law keeps the prairies for
the Indians and for us who are their sons. Their law
gives the prairie to everyone.

ANDRE:
You cannot hold up history, my son. God would not
want you to try. Two years ago when we made our
rules, there was no law on the prairie. With the
Mounted Police, the law has come, and we must
obey it.

DUMONT:
Even if the law robs us, Father?

ANDRE:
If the law robs us, we must try to change it, but if
we do not succeed, we must obey, trusting in God
that justice will in the end prevail.

Scene Four

DUMONT:
>We obeyed — and the law robbed us. Under its protection the hunters came from outside and swept the buffalo from the prairie. The Indians saw their way of life was ended; they signed the treaties that made them starving pensioners. The railway probed like a steel snake out of the east; it helped the English farmers on their journey to the Saskatchewan. But no one was content, for the new law did not act like a law, since it protected only the rapacious, and even the men who came from Canada and England seeking land and space found themselves the victims of speculators. As for my people, the Métis, our lands were invaded by surveyors who spoke neither French nor Cree. They tried to arrange our long river farms into squares, with no guarantee that the squares would belong to us in the end. Injustice, monsieur, encourages strange friendships. And when the Métis and the Indians and the English half breeds and the Canadian settlers had all sent their appeals to Ottawa without any result, their patience came to an end, and as the rivers broke free and the roads became clear again in the spring, we began to talk to each other of our troubles. On the sixth of May we all gathered in the schoolhouse at Lindsay and there we reached the decision that has made me in the end your prisoner.

JACKSON: *his voice gradually becoming audible*
>Gentlemen, we have all reached the ends of our various tethers. We have come to the point where persuasion has failed, not because it has been refuted, but because it had not even been considered. The government in Ottawa has used against us the strategy of the deaf ear, and against that strategy words are useless. We must act, and if we are to act we must be led by a man of action.

ISBISTER:

If we need a man of action, let us elect Gabriel Dumont to be the leader of us all! I propose it on behalf of the English half-breeds.

There is applause.

DUMONT:

Thank you, Mr. Isbister. But, for myself, I oppose Gabriel Dumont!

Laughter is heard.

I am not joking, my friends. I oppose this nomination because I am not the kind of man you need for the task you have to do. If you wanted someone to lead a hunting party or lay an ambush or even to fight a little battle, then I would be your man. But I do not have the gift to carry on talks with ministers and parliaments. I cannot write and I am too old to learn. The man we need must write well and know the minds of politicians.

NOLIN:

Gabriel is right. We all esteem his good qualities, one of which is that he knows his limitations. There is one man — and one man only, who can help us — Louis Riel!

There are noises of agitation and shouts of "Hear! Hear!" and "No!"

ISBISTER:

Mr. Nolin, have you forgotten that in the minds of many Canadians the name of Louis Riel spells out rebellion and murder?

NOLIN:

Riel never acted unconstitutionally, he was never legally a rebel, and the one man killed on the Red River while Riel ruled died by judicial progress. And if Riel's name does frighten some people, perhaps that will be a good thing. They will know then that we mean business.

JACKSON:

I can speak for the Settlers' Union, and we are all Canadians and English. But I can see no one but Louis Riel to whom we can turn for help. Have you any alternative to suggest, Mr. Isbister?

ISBISTER:

None, I confess, Mr. Jackson. I am not opposed to Riel, and if you decide to call on him I shall not make difficulties. But in making our decision we should be aware of the problems. That is all I meant to say.

NOLIN:

I believe that the idea of Riel and the problems connected with him have been in all our minds for some time now. They have been in mine, and I have reached my own decision as many of you must have done.

There are shouts of "Hear! Hear!"

I therefore propose that we invite Riel to come as our adviser, and with the chairman's permission I would like to put to the meeting this resolution: "We, the French and English natives of the North-west, knowing that Louis Riel made a bargain with the Government of Canada in 1870, which said bargain is contained in what is known as the 'Manitoba Act,' have thought it advisable that a delegation be sent to said Louis Riel and . . ."

His voice fades out.

Scene Five

DUMONT:

So it was decided to call on Louis Riel and our delegation was chosen. There was Mr. Isbister, and Michel Dumas, and I was the third, while Moise Ouellete decided to accompany us for the pleasure of the journey. It was a year ago that we followed the deserted trails of the migrant Indians south from Batoche. We rode seven hundred miles. When we began, the first crocuses were breaking the earth. It was the year after the buffalo vanished. Their bones lay thick in the ungrazed grass, and for the first spring in my memory the ground was not shaken by the thunder of their hooves. Our west had ended. We were looking for a man who could make us another. On the first day of June we crossed the border. On the fourth day our journey ended at St. Peter's Mission. We rode beside the Sun River between the log huts of our Métis brethren and the lodges of the Blackfoot. It was a Sunday.

The tinny tolling of a Mission bell is heard.

DUMAS:

There's the school where he teaches, on the river bank beside the church. He lives in the hut beyond it.

ISBISTER:

A wretched hovel for the founder of Manitoba! They've certainly hunted Riel to a desolate end of the earth!

DUMONT:

No end for him or for us, James Isbister, if I can help it!

ISBISTER:

Let's go over and see if he's home.

DUMONT:

No need. There he is, coming out of the church. Yes, he's changed in fifteen years. Heavy and bearded! The years have gnawed at him. And yet the way he looks at us! That is Riel! Bonjour, Louis Riel!

RIEL:

Dumont! Uncle Gabriel! As welcome as your archangel namesake!

DUMONT:

Wait for your welcome to hear what we want. We have come to call you back to your past. The Métis need you again.

ISBISTER:

We need you also, Mr. Riel.

RIEL:

You, monsieur? I do not think . . .

DUMONT:

This is James Isbister. He speaks for the English half-breeds of the Saskatchewan. You know the others — Michel Dumas — Moise Ouellette . . .

RIEL:

I remember them. Welcome, mes amis! And I remember your family from the Red River, Mr. Isbister. What do you want with me, messieurs?

DUMONT:

All that you gave the Métis half a lifetime ago when you ruled Fort Garry.

RIEL:

That was a hollow reign, Gabriel. Time has swept it away like the mists that hovered over the river this morning.

ISBISTER:

And yet you won their rights for the Red River people, Mr. Riel.

RIEL:

If that is the case, monsieur, why did you leave the Red River to seek a new home farther west? I can tell you. It is because whatever I won for the Métis was lost when the Canadian settlers surged into Manitoba and the moon of the hunter set for ever.

DUMONT:

Fifteen years ago we could have stopped them. We could have ambushed the redcoats at the portages. I warned you not to let them enter, Louis.

RIEL:

We had given our word to join the Dominion. I meant to keep it.

DUMONT:

Did they keep theirs? No! Macdonald sent an army to make us his subjects — the lesser people who spoke no English!

RIEL:

You did nothing to help us, Gabriel.

DUMONT:

I was on the prairie, awaiting your call. If it had come I would have brought five hundred marksmen. The Indian chiefs of the Lake of the Woods were waiting also. You never called us.

RIEL:

I did not want bloodshed.

DUMONT:

You killed one man. That was enough.

RIEL:

His death was justified. Thomas Scott, the fool and braggart, the Orangeman's mind sealed in by prejudice! His own kind loathed him!

DUMONT:

Until he was dead, and then they loved him. You might have killed a hundred good men and been no more hated.

ISBISTER:

Gabriel Dumont, we have not travelled seven hundred miles to relive a dead year. This is 1884 and our problems are in the Northwest, not in Fort Garry.

DUMONT:

Our friend is right. You and I, Louis, may disagree on some points, but no other man could have done what you did. And then you went into exile, driven by rulers who broke their pledges. Without you we lost what you had won, but we clung to the faith and pride you had given us. We moved westward as the game moved, and in the green hills by a new river we followed the hunt like our fathers while the buffalo lasted, returning with our Red River carts screaming under the weight of pemmican and dried meat, and robes for the winter. We built our churches and when the buffalo dwindled we cut our farms from the prairie in strips of land running back from the river, as you remember them.

RIEL:

Can I ever forget them? The farms we tried to save from the hands of Canadian strangers beside the Red River!

DUMONT:

> The strangers have followed us on to other rivers.
> They are taking the lands we held by the natural
> right of the sons of Indians. For ten years we have
> petitioned Ottawa. We have pleaded for titles, called
> for protection. All we have heard is silence.

ISBISTER:

> Whether we are English or French, halfbreed or
> white, the land thieves threaten us all. That is why
> we decided to act together.

RIEL:

> What can you do by acting together, or by acting
> alone for that matter?

DUMONT:

> Did you ask that question on the Red River?

RIEL:

> Yes, and answered it, as you know very well.

ISBISTER:

> Which is why we have come to you, Mr. Riel. You
> made a bargain in 1870 with the Government of
> Canada. We need a bargain now, and we think you
> can help us to get it by your experience and your
> knowledge.

RIEL:

> The French and the English are in it together, you
> say?

ISBISTER:

> The English are as angry as the French.

RIEL:

> Then times have really changed, Mr. Isbister. But so
> has my life. I was a subject of Queen Victoria in 1869.
> Now I am an American, and Canada is a foreign land
> to me.

DUMONT:

> The Métis are the same, Louis, everywhere and always. The frontier means nothing to us. We owe our loyalties only to those who treat us justly.

RIEL:

> I have no longer only myself to think of.

DUMONT:

> We will look after your family.

RIEL:

> What is the date today?

ISBISTER:

> The fourth of June.

RIEL:

> And there are four of you.

ISBISTER:

> Yes — but what of it?

RIEL:

> I must have a day to pray and decide. One more day . . .

Scene Six

RIEL:

> Gentlemen, today is the fifth of June. And we are five. The conjunction is fortunate. It is propitious to my mission.

ISBISTER:

> Your mission, sir? What does that mean?

RIEL:

All my life I have been conscious of a mission. The voice of God spoke to me on a hilltop far away in Massachusetts. He gave me the name of David, slayer of giants. After I left Fort Garry with a price on my head, I thought my purpose in life had ended. When God spoke I knew it had hardly begun. But I did not know that immediately. At first I had doubts. Perhaps — I thought — the Devil had spoken. But the Bishop knew it was God's voice.

DUMONT:

Which bishop, Louis?

RIEL:

The Bishop who, through my actions, will become Pope! Bishop Bourget of Montreal! Look! This is what he wrote to me. "God has always directed you. He has given you a mission which must be completed in every way." Here is the letter, Gabriel. The Bishop's signature! The Bishop's seal!

DUMAS:

It is the Bishop's seal!

RIEL:

Gentlemen, my mission takes me by your paths. My mission is to return to my people and lead them into Zion. Gabriel Dumont, here is my answer.

DUMONT:

You could have saved your ink, Louis. I speak six languages well enough for men to listen to me — all the languages of the prairies except English. But I read none of them. The hunter needs nothing more than a good memory.

RIEL:

Memory dies with the rememberer, Gabriel. We are acting for history. I will tell you what is written. I also have claims in Canada, for land not given, for a stipend not paid when I kept the peace in Red River, for compensation for the agonies of exile. I will make our plea together. Let us go now, and when the poplars turn golden I shall return here, to the mission. Here also I must work among our people. Gentlemen, let us pray. O Father, thy providence is boundless and beautiful. Bless me according to it. Amen.

THE OTHERS:

Amen.

There is a long, silent pause.

RIEL:

Gabriel, what do you see? There, on the hill, what do you see?

DUMONT:

I see only a pine tree that the lightning has splintered.

RIEL:

I see a gallows, and I am swinging from it.

Scene Seven

DUMONT:

Three days afterwards we left the mission and rode north over the plains to the poplared valley where our villages lay. The spring had ended. The July sun was withering the grasses on the prairie. The yellow dust announced our coming, and as we neared Batoche the people rode out, dancing their horses, cheering and firing.

The beat of hooves, the crack of muskets and the shouting of "Vive Riel! Vive Dumont!" are heard.

Louis Riel, your people welcome you!

RIEL:
So they have not forgotten!

DUMONT:
They will always remember. But now there is no time for memory. Mes amis! Mes amis!

The background hubbub dies away.

This is a great day for the Métis. We have brought our leader home.

There is cheering, subsiding as Dumont shouts in competition.

Many of you — many of you once carried your guns under Louis Riel's command. You triumphed with him and with him you were defrauded of your victory. Now he has listened to our call and has come back to live among us for a little while. He will give us a voice to speak to the government. They did not listen to us, but he will open their ears, as he did before.

There are cries of "Welcome Louis Riel! Long live the Nation of the Métis!" all subsiding as Riel begins to speak, with emotion.

RIEL:
Compatriots of the prairie, your welcome leaves me without words. I treasure your welcome, your friendship, and pray that I may serve you.

More cheering is heard.

NOLIN:

Louis! Louis! Have you forgotten your own cousin?

RIEL:

Charles Nolin! Cousin Charles! I have every reason to forget you. At Red River you opposed me. You played safe with the Company. You played safe with the Canadians. While I suffered in exile you prospered. You became a minister in the province I founded, while I wandered with a price on my head instead of a roof.

NOLIN:

That's all in the past, Louis. I've learnt there are no spoons long enough to sup with the Ottawa devils. In Batoche you and I are on the same side.

DUMONT:

It is true. Your cousin insisted on calling you here.

RIEL:

Here's my hand then, Cousin Charles.

NOLIN:

My house is yours. Make it your home and your headquarters.

RIEL:

I accept. I thank you, for my family most of all. They need rest.

NOLIN:

You are tired too. Let us go. You will need your strength.

RIEL:

No! No! I see so many old companions! I must speak to them all!

DUMONT:

You will have time for that, Louis!

ISBISTER:

> Stay at least a moment, Mr. Riel, to meet a man who
> has come a long way to greet you. This is Will Jackson
> from Prince Albert. He is the secretary of the Settlers'
> Union. He speaks for the English and Canadian
> farmers.

RIEL:

> I am enchanted to meet you, Mr. Jackson.

JACKSON:

> We remember what you did in Manitoba, Mr. Riel;
> how you united the people there and forced open the
> mean hand of Macdonald. Sir John is misruling us
> again, and we must unite as we did before.

RIEL:

> You think as I do, Mr. Jackson! A banner of
> friendship like a sky sheltering the prairies! Men from
> every corner of the world living beneath it in peace,
> secure from tyranny! It is my mission to bring that
> world into being by the grace of God working
> through my voice. There will be a new heaven and
> a new earth, and to prepare for them there will be a
> new church and a new Pope here on the prairies,
> under the Northern Lights . . .

NOLIN:

> What are you saying, cousin? A new Pope! If Father
> André hears of that . . .

RIEL:

> Let Father André hear what he hears. I speak of what
> will come.

DUMONT:

> No doubt it will come, Louis. And when it does there
> will be no harm if the priests dislike it. But first we
> must do what has to be done. We must protect the
> rights of the people who live here between one crop
> of grass and another. We must act. You came here to
> act.

RIEL:

> Vision and action need each other, Gabriel. You are the man who acts.

JACKSON:

> You are the man who sees, Mr. Riel. You are the prophet, I recognise you.

RIEL:

> You see, Gabriel, Mr. Jackson is the third of us, the man who hears and understands. We are hands and eyes and ears, and together we shall conquer.

DUMONT:

> Hands and eyes and ears are not enough. Before we have finished we shall need guns and horses. How many can you muster, Mr. Jackson? How many of the great English talkers will come with their guns when the fighting starts?

RIEL:

> There will be no guns and bloodshed, Gabriel! This is God's fight. We shall start tomorrow, gather the people as we did long ago, call our meetings, elect our officers, and hunt for justice as once we hunted the giant vanished beasts of the prairies!

Scene Eight

DUMONT:

> The months gnawed at my patience. We wandered from meeting to meeting through the dusty summer until the leaves fell and the geese flew south and the land turned iron under our horses' hooves. Riel did not go back, and we dreamed of a great alliance. The English cheered when he spoke. The Indian chiefs came secretly to meet him. Their people were starving and yearning for lost gods. In November,

84

we completed our petition to Ottawa, and gathered
to consider how we should present it.

> *There is a buzz of voices, fading behind*
> *JACKSON as he begins to speak.*

JACKSON:
The English half-breeds and the Settlers' Union have
accepted your ideas, gentlemen. Here is the final
draft.

NOLIN:
What does it ask for, Mr. Jackson?

JACKSON:
Something for everyone. A land grant for the Métis
and the half-breeds, recognizing their claims as the
children of Indians; for the Indians themselves more
land, more food, more freedom; for the white settlers
immediate titles to land and protection from
speculators; for all of us a provincial government,
members in Ottawa, reduced tariffs, a railway to
Hudson's Bay, and control over our lands. If it is
granted, there will be no need for further action.
The prairies will be at peace.

NOLIN:
I do not see how we can fail. Our terms are just. We
are united. Louis Riel's name has worked its magic,
and only fools can ignore us.

RIEL:
Fools and rascals, cousin. The same man sits in
Ottawa as sat there fifteen years ago. Old Tomorrow
— and Old Yesterday! And from the Manitoba he
founded, the Métis have departed, you among them,
because their life was made impossible to endure.

DUMONT:
Do you mean, Louis Riel, that after all these months
of talk our petition is useless?

RIEL:

It states our demands for history, Gabriel. It warns the government and they have to be warned. But no one can say that it will have any effect. There are a hundred ways for politicians to evade doing what is right. Corruption is one of them. They have tried it with me.

DUMONT:

With you, Louis?

RIEL:

With me. Because they themselves are venial they think others have their prices. They offered me a place in the Territorial Council. They whispered about the Senate. When I refused both, they talked of money.

DUMONT:

And that also you refused?

RIEL:

I did not. They owe me money. It is my right. But I asked for more than I knew they would give! A hundred thousand dollars! That was a surprise for them! They did not agree!

He laughs rather wildly; for a moment the others are silent.

DUMONT:

Well, they've tried bribery. What next?

NOLIN:

The priests are saying that Macdonald will send more policemen. They are saying he will send soldiers rather than grant our demands.

DUMONT:

> We shall have time to think of that. Their railway is not ready. Perhaps it never will be. Give me a thousand men, and I can destroy it and lay such ambushes that not a single soldier will get within a hundred miles of Batoche.

RIEL:

> There will be no ambushes because there will be no soldiers. They will use the priests against us.

NOLIN:

> The priests claim they are protecting us.

DUMONT:

> The priests love power and those who wield it.

RIEL:

> The priests hate me.

NOLIN:

> Why should they hate you, Louis?

RIEL:

> Because God has chosen me and rejected them. Rome is ended and the old world is dying. In this land I shall build a new world and a new church and within it Catholic and Protestant and Jew and Christian shall be united and equal. Bishop Bourget shall be its Pope, and Gabriel Dumont will be its general, and I shall be its prophet. Never again will just men be forced to wander, and the Métis nation will flourish under the bright sky of the future.

NOLIN:

> A splendid vision, cousin. But while we wait for it to be fulfilled, is it worth the trouble of sending our petition? Or is that perhaps too trivial for people with such a future?

RIEL:

> We shall send it because we must give the men in Ottawa the choice of whether to do evil or good.

DUMONT:

> And if they decide to do nothing more than ignore us, what shall we do then?

RIEL:

> God will hold them responsible for the agony and the rage.

Scene Nine

DUMONT:

> The winter deepened, the storms beat on our houses, and above the white hills the gods of our Indian mothers spoke in the crackling sky. Out of the east came only silence. Weathercocks veered. The faint-hearted grew fainter. This year dawned, and when February came those who were desperate had drawn near to the edge of desperate action. The Indians talked of war. I carried it in my heart. Then came the messages that promised nothing. Late that month we all gathered at Batoche.

> *A hubbub of voices, dying down, is heard.*

RIEL:

> At last the government has spoken. Charles Nolin has received a message. I request him to read it to you.

NOLIN:

> Do not prepare to cheer, my friends. Nothing is granted and nothing is promised. We are to be counted by the census takers and an investigation of our claims will soon begin. Mark the word *soon*. Not now! That is all.

DUMAS:

What has Louis Riel to say about this?

There are shouts of "Riel! Riel!" which subside as he begins to speak.

RIEL:

People of the Métis nation, all I have to say is "Farewell."

There are shouts of "No!" and a hubbub of exclamation.

I do not say it without reason, my friends. Three seasons have drifted away since you called me and I answered. I have lived among you. I have encouraged you. I have advised. I have defended your cause. And I call you and God to witness that I have asked you for nothing. What you offered I accepted because I thought my name and experience would bring you justice. My name has been useless. The reply was sent to my cousin Charles Nolin because the men in Ottawa wish to forget that I have ever existed. So it is not a message for me. It is a message for you, my people. And what does it say to you? It says that possession rests with the powerful, that the Canadians will take our lands on the Saskatchewan as they did on the Red River, and that nothing is to be won by persuasion. I came here to persuade. I did my best, and I have failed. I am not a citizen of this country, and my past has weighed us all down. There is no reason for me to stay. I shall go. I shall leave tomorrow.

Shouts of "No!", "You Shall Not go!" are heard amid a general agitation; as it subsides, RIEL speaks again.

Why do you want to keep me? There is nothing left for me to do.

DUMAS:

>We called you, Louis Riel, because you were our only hope. If you do not stay, we shall have no hope, and all we can do is follow you into exile.

RIEL:

>Have you thought of the consequences if I stay? Macdonald answered as he did because I, Louis Riel, am hated by the English. If I go, the government may give you better terms.

DUMONT:

>It will never give us better terms unless we show our strength.

RIEL:

>If I stay things will continue as they are going, and we shall have to find new means of persuasion, Uncle Gabriel.

DUMONT:

>I have always been ready to use other means of persuasion. Stay, and we will welcome the consequences!

>*The crowd cheers.*

RIEL:

>You may have to follow me along the edge of an abyss. Are you willing to do that?

>*There are shouts of "Yes!".*

>Then I will stay with you, my compatriots, and Ottawa shall hear my answer.

Scene Ten

DUMONT:

> We had reached the hour when the hunter lifts his
> gun, rides through the herd and hopes by luck or skill
> to kill his beast and save his life. Once the dust rises
> from the pounding hooves and the bulls charge, there
> is no choice except to forget your fear. Whether
> Riel saw all that was against us I never knew. I saw
> some of it myself, yet I went on as I did in the old
> days, riding into the heart of the turmoil. It was in
> March that the priests showed their hands against
> us. . . .

ANDRE:

> Ever since you came here, Louis Riel, you have been
> preaching against the church and the Holy Father.
> And now you ask me for my support. I must know
> your intentions first.

RIEL:

> On the Red River the priests were with us, Father
> André. They were Métis and they acted like brothers
> in race and spirit.

ANDRE:

> And I am not a Métis. Is that what you mean? Race
> means nothing in the eye of God, my son. The
> welfare of your people has always been dearer to me
> than my own. Their grievances are just, and I will
> support just action to remove them.

RIEL:

> We have tried everything to gain our rights. We have
> sent letters and petitions and telegrams . . .

ANDRE:

> I also have sent my warnings to the blind men in
> Ottawa.

DUMONT:

>You have succeeded no better than we have, Father. It is time we did something new. It is time we acted for ourselves as you and I did years ago when we established the council of the Métis to rule in St. Laurent.

ANDRE:

>Be careful, Gabriel, my son. What could be done twelve years ago may not be possible now. You may end by destroying yourselves.

RIEL:

>I have a way of asserting peacefully the rights of men whose protests have gone unheard. I shall establish a provisional government, as I did fifteen years ago on the Red River. Everyone from the whites to the Indians will have a voice. You must support me, Father.

ANDRE:

>My sons, you are both living in the past. In sixty-nine there was no government on the Red River. In seventy-three there was no government in Saskatchewan. Each time a void existed. You filled it in your way, Louis, and you in yours, Gabriel. This time there is a government. If you form your own government you will be rebels, and the church does not condone rebellion. And even if we did support you, how could we possibly succeed? There are thousands of us. There are millions of them.

DUMONT:

>If I give the sign, Father, the Indians will rise from the Red River to the Rockies, and the Sioux will ride north over the border!

ANDRE:

>So you are planning an Indian war, Gabriel Dumont?

RIEL:

> We do not need the Indians, Father. I have only to beckon and a multitude of people who fear God will join me!

ANDRE:

> Where will they come from in time to save you? My sons, neither of you sees the world as it is. You, Gabriel, are hankering after the old life of the prairie, but the death of the buffalo will prevent your ever returning. And you, Louis Riel, have filled your mind with heretical utopias which can never be fulfilled. Go home, humble yourselves, and pray for guidance!

RIEL:

> Father André, I thought of you as a man of God. I find you are a traitor to the people you came to serve. No matter. I shall establish my government. I shall show my power, and woe to him who opposes me!

DUMONT:

> Priest, your day is ended. The people no longer trust you!

Scene Eleven

DUMONT:

> The priests refused us the sacrament, and Riel cursed them in the church of St. Anthony. After that we rode over the countryside, gathering our supporters. On the eighteenth of March we returned to Batoche and rode through the village with sixty mounted men. Nobody then knew what we would do, for none of us had the desire to fire the first shot. It was Charles Nolin who threw the match into the powder barrel.

NOLIN:

Louis! Louis! I have news for you!

RIEL:

What is your news, Cousin Charles?

NOLIN:

You must all disperse. You, Louis, must run for the border. Everything is finished!

DUMONT:

What do you mean by finished, Charles Nolin?

NOLIN:

The police are sending reinforcements. They will arrest us.

DUMONT:

Who told you that?

NOLIN:

Laurence Clarke, the Hudson's Bay man.

DUMONT:

Clarke told you that! And Clarke is in the government. If Clarke says the police are coming, I think he knows.

NOLIN:

It will be war if you do not give in!

RIEL:

Who will give in? Will you give in, Uncle Gabriel?

DUMONT:

Never!

RIEL:

Will anyone give in?

There are shouts of "No!" "Never!"

94

That is our answer to the police and their masters. They have decided on force, and now we can use it against them. They have freed our hands to pick up the rifle. The time has come, my friends! Meet at the church! Call the people together! To arms!

> *The shouting of "Aux Armes!" mingles with the sound of horses riding away, and then the churchbell, tolling the tocsin and fading out.*

ANDRE:

You shall not enter the house of God, Louis Riel!

RIEL:

I speak with the voice of God! His house is mine. We are at war. The government has chosen. We shall occupy the church to carry on our holy struggle. Out of my way, priest!

ANDRE:

You are a heretic! I protest against your crossing this threshold!

RIEL:

Listen to the priest! He is protesting! He has become a Protestant!

ANDRE:

If you insist on coming in, I shall remove God's body from your presence!

RIEL:

Take your monstrance and go! Rome has fallen, my people. God's folk are entering God's house! Let the priests stay away! My friends, the government has answered your petitions! It is sending more police!

> *There is an angry hubbub.*

But I do not recognize their police! You are my police.

Applause greets this speech.

DUMONT:
>I propose the Provisional Government.

Applause follows.

RIEL:
>The Provisional Government is approved by acclamation and is hereby established. Let us nominate the members.

DUMAS:
>For President I nominate Louis Riel!

More applause greets this.

RIEL:
>I thank you for your choice. You have not forgotten the days of Red River. But I do not accept. I will remain your prophet and nothing more. God did not give me the name of David for nothing.

DUMAS:
>If you will not be our leader, who will?

RIEL:
>The flock shall lead itself. We will pick a council of twelve, all of them equal with each other and with the rest of you. We will call them Exovedes, which means those from the flock, and the council will be called the Exovedate.

There is a murmur of puzzled discussion.

DUMONT:
>I am not a learned man, Louis, and the name means nothing to me, and I do not think it means anything to the rest of us. The idea of a council is a good one. But we are at war, and war is like the buffalo hunt.

It needs good leadership. When the buffalo ran
we chose a chief every year. No one challenged his
word. Now we shall be hunting the Mounted Police.
For that also we need a chief.

DUMAS:

You were the chief of our hunts, Gabriel.

RIEL:

Then let us name Gabriel Dumont the Adjutant
General of the Métis nation.

There is applause.

DUMONT:

You have named me. I accept, and now you will hear
my orders. I defer only to Louis Riel. First we will
pick ten captains, as we did in the old days. Then we
will ride out and cut the telegraph lines, capture the
arms and ammunition in the trading posts, and seize
as hostages all men in our villages who are not Métis,
except for the priests, and the priests we will watch.
We will send our messengers to the English half-
breeds and to the Indians. The government will see
that we do not go to sleep when we are threatened.
Perhaps that will persuade them to give us what we
ask for, and if it does not we shall show what the free
men of the prairies can do!

More applause follows.

Scene Twelve

DUMONT:

For a few days it was like the still hours before a
storm. The English half-breeds hid their arms, sent
us their best wishes and stayed at home, waiting to
see what would happen. The Indian chiefs, Big Bear

and Poundmaker, went on the warpath. Inspector Crozier, the police chief at Fort Carlton, sent a messenger calling us for a parley. Riel sent a message calling on Crozier to surrender. We did not fulfill our threat. He waited for reinforcements. We waited for the Indians, but only a few of them came to us. On the twenty-fifth of March I seized the government stores at Duck Lake. The next day a police patrol came to fetch them. We were too strong for them, and they went back. It was our first victory, without blood, and some of us were foolish enough to believe we had won the war. I knew Crozier would not accept defeat, and I was not surprised when our scouts came to say that the police were approaching in strength. Crozier came marching through the snow from Fort Carlton with a hundred men and a little brass cannon. We had time to prepare a surprise for the police, with our men behind bushes, and sharpshooters in a little hut overlooking the trail. But we did not want to kill them like animals without warning, and we tried to parley. There was no good will. The police fired first, and my brother Isidore was killed.

> *A single shot is heard as he pronounces the word "killed," followed by a patter of rifle fire in the background, continuing throughout the scene.*

The battle started and my heart leapt, for this was the real struggle and the end of the sham war of words. At first we were few, but Riel came with a hundred horsemen. He was unarmed, but in his hand he waved a crucifix taken from the church.

RIEL:
> In the name of God the Father, fight for justice, purify the land!

DUMONT:
> Let us make the redcoats jump, men! Keep your cover and make every bullet count!

He ends in a gasp of agony.

DUMAS:

Gabriel! He is shot in the head! Help him!

DUMONT:

It is nothing, Michel! Leave me alone . . . they've grooved my scalp . . . my head's too hard for English bullets . . . no time to worry now . . . Delorme, advance to the cabin on the left! Open fire on their flank. Boyer, creep through the wood and hold your fire till you reach the top of the hillock. Then pick them out from above!

> *For a moment the sound of firing is loud and goes on without interruption.*

Look! The fools have jammed their cannon! Ouelette, take twenty men to the other side of the cabin. It's time to surround them and finish them off!

RIEL:

Forward my brave ones, in the name of the Holy Spirit!

DUMAS:

They're not waiting to be surrounded! They're running away!

> *The fire becomes sporadic.*

RIEL:

The Lord has given us victory!

DUMONT:

With the help of a little good shooting!

RIEL:

His wisdom directed your hands and eyes! Let us now give praise!

DUMONT:

> Let us do that later. Now we must pursue them and kill them off!

RIEL:

> Let them go, Gabriel! Look at the dead men, and all the blood on the snow like the writing of doom! Enough has been shed. God showed his hand in our victory, and even Macdonald cannot ignore such a sign!

DUMONT:

> It would have been a better sign if we had made our victory complete!

RIEL:

> Let them go, Gabriel! Glorify our cause with mercy. Let us return to our homes, praising God who has protected them!

Scene Thirteen

DUMONT:

> It was when the winter began to break that we had news of the Canadians. They came more quickly than we thought, travelling on the stretches of new railway and going by sleigh in the gaps. They were on the prairies when the rivers broke free. We were too simple. We did not believe vengeance could descend so quickly, and under Louis' influence we lived in the hope of miracles and were willing to forget that death was near. So we did not do all we might have done or all that even then I knew we should do. We talked of eternity and time was the question.

RIEL:

> Fellow councillors and Exovedes, let us return today to planning the new dispensation. God inspires me

to talk of Hell. No-one can deny that Hell exists. The
priests tell us that it will continue to exist for ever.
But it is possible to conceive that a God of boundless
mercy can decree an unending punishment?

DUMONT:

You are right, Louis, but if Hell exists it will
carry on for a little while, and we can decide to
abolish it in a month or two. The question now is
how long Batoche can carry on if we do not decide
how to act at this moment. I have a message from
Jerome Henry. He drives a team for General
Middleton and he is also one of our scouts.
Middleton is marching north from Qu'Appelle. He
has nearly two thousand men and many cannon.
We must decide now how we are going to stop him.

RIEL:

God will give us the sign, Gabriel. He will tell us how
to act, and when.

DUMONT:

God works through men, Louis. On the buffalo hunt
we never waited for the game to search us out. We
sought them, and God blessed our diligence.

RIEL:

What do we need that God has not provided?

DUMONT:

More men. More arms. More ammunition. And more
deeds. We have three hundred and fifty men, not all
of them trustworthy. Only two hundred have guns
that fire. Let us call the Métis in Fort Edmonton
and Montana to join us. Let us persuade the
Blackfoot to take the warpath. Let us keep the
enemy from Batoche by fighting them like wolves
attacking elk, biting their flanks and heels but never
facing the charge. We are too few to fight battles, but
we can win ambushes, we can attack by night and
capture rifles, we can stampede their horses, we can

set the prairie on fire, we can pot them one by one, and wear the survivors down to cowardice. We can ride southward and blow up the railway to cut them off.

RIEL:

There must be no night attacks, Uncle Gabriel.

DUMONT:

They are our only chance. Then we can meet the enemy with everything in our favour, and at the end of three nights I will make them so jumpy that they will fight each other, not us.

RIEL:

That is an Indian way of fighting, Gabriel. We are not Indians.

DUMONT:

We are the sons of Indians. What else do you propose to do?

RIEL:

God will reveal how things shall come to be. Do not ask when, but he will destroy our foes. Until that time there must be no more bloodshed.

DUMONT:

Does God tell you that we need not fight?

RIEL:

When the time comes, we shall fight.

DUMONT:

Backs to the wall, in Batoche, against a fresh and well-armed enemy!

RIEL:

God acts through miracles.

DUMONT:

God gives chances. And who is to say when a chance is not a miracle? Every nightfall, every gulch and coulée is a chance, and we should use it to wear the enemy away.

RIEL:

Until God gives us a sign we dare not.

DUMONT:

You talked of war and blood, Louis, until we were at war. Now you want to fight and not to fight. And the rest of you are all silent.

A man coughs uneasily.

You are silent because you are afraid to speak against our prophet Louis, and you are ashamed to refuse to fight. Pray hard, my friends! We shall need it!

Scene Fourteen

DUMONT:

Day after day Middleton advanced at his leisure, and in Batoche we argued and did nothing. At last the Canadians camped twenty-two miles from Batoche. That night I confronted Riel.

DUMONT:

In two days, if we don't stop them, Louis, the redcoats will be in Batoche. We *must* stop them. If we let them carry out all their plans, we shall be caught like buffalo in a pound. There will be no chance to defend ourselves or even to escape.

RIEL:

God has not yet given the sign.

DUMONT:

We wait for God! We wait for the Indians! We wait
for Middleton! My men are impatient, and every day
they get more nervous. If we do nothing, they will
begin to melt away because they will lose faith in us
all.

RIEL:

Faith in men is always misplaced.

DUMONT:

God helps those who have faith in themselves.
Whatever you say now, I plan to ambush the redcoats
in Tourond's Coulée. We will give them such a
stinging that they will not attack Batoche in a hurry!

RIEL:

Are your men with you in that?

DUMONT:

Yes, but if we do nothing now I will not vouch for
them.

RIEL:

Very well. Do as you wish, Gabriel, and God go with
you.

Scene Fifteen

DUMONT: *the Métis "Song of Pierre Falcon" sounding
softly in the background to his narration* You have
already heard, Monsieur le Commandant, what
happened at Tourond's Coulée, which the English
call Fish Creek. I planned it all like a buffalo pound.
We would let them get into the coulée, and then we
would shoot them down from all sides. There were
150 of us and 800 of them. We went to Tourond's
Farm and killed a bull and some chickens for our

breakfast, and when our scout, Gilbert Bréland, came
to tell us that the enemy was approaching, I thought
I had him in my trap. I put a special bullet in my gun
for that old bull buffalo, General Middleton. But
some of our young men rode over the trail through
Tourond's Coulée, and the English scouts saw their
tracks. So Middleton was on his guard, and yet in
spite of their numbers and their cannon, we held the
redcoats in the gulley until evening, and we blooded
them well, for there were many dead. For two weeks
they licked the wounds where we had mauled them.
Then on the seventh of May they marched to my
ferry over the Saskatchewan, which men call Gabriel's
Crossing. They tore down my stable and burnt my
house. They stole my billiard table.

In Batoche we heard that Poundmaker and his
Assiniboines and Crees had beaten the English outside
Battleford. We expected him to march to our aid, but
though we sent messengers, the Indians never arrived,
nor did the Métis from Montana and Fort Edmonton.
We faced the redcoats alone. On the ninth of May
they reached Batoche. We fought four long and bitter
days. Old men and boys lay in the rifle pits beside the
hunters. I was beside Joseph Ouelette, aged ninety-
three, and his courage kept me at my post until an
English bullet killed him and I thanked him and
departed. Women picked bullets from the ground for
their men to use again. At the end we were firing
stones and nails from our muskets while the powder
lasted. Riel foretold victory, and all the time he
prayed for it, and there was victory, but we did not
win. Our men died in the rifle pits or crept away
when their powder ran out, and the priests were there
with whispers of surrender. On the twelfth of May it
was all ended, and white flags flew over Batoche like
captive doves. It was then that I saw Riel for the last
time. He was in a wood, trying in vain to persuade a
few men to keep fighting.

RIEL:

My voice has lost its power. My people are scattered and those who are with me do not hear what I say.

DUMONT:

They know it is the end. Batoche is finished, Louis. And there is nowhere else to make a stand. You know what the English say. "He who fights and runs away, lives to fight another day." There is a time to fight and a time to run. To stay here is death.

RIEL:

You are telling me we are beaten.

DUMONT:

Napoleon himself could not fight without men or bullets.

RIEL:

Beaten! Defeated! I cannot believe it.

DUMONT:

When you talked of war and we took up arms, you should have thought of that, Louis. I knew from the beginning that two sides cannot win the same battle.

RIEL:

Why did you fight, then?

DUMONT:

Defeat seemed better than submission. There was a chance, and I was content with a chance.

RIEL:

God spoke to me, Gabriel. I know he spoke.

DUMONT:

You may have misunderstood him.

RIEL:

What can we do now?

DUMONT:

I know what I shall do. I have ninety cartridges and I am a dead shot. I shall stay in the woods and pick off the redcoats when they come to hunt me. When my ammunition is finished I shall go south like a migrant bird.

RIEL:

I have lived for years with a price on my head, and I do not want to continue. It would mock my mission.

DUMONT:

We are beaten, Louis, and you still talk of a mission!

RIEL:

Where God points, I must follow. The saints did not ask for a safe journey.

DUMONT:

You are telling me that you mean to surrender.

RIEL:

Yes!

DUMONT:

They will hang you if they catch you.

RIEL:

If they want to hang me, they have to try me. That is the law of the English. And they have to try me in public. I shall make the court my platform. I shall expose our sorrows to the final sigh, and so I shall fulfill my mission.

DUMONT:

Before you do anything that cannot be changed, think of what I am saying.

RIEL:

I am listening.

DUMONT:

> When I went to St. Peter's Mission with the others
> who are not with us any more, I persuaded you to
> come from safety into danger. Let me take you back
> by the secret Indian trails from danger into safety.
> Then we can stay among the Americans until the
> wind changes and the weather is friendly to us. If
> you want to come, meet me here tonight at sunset,
> or the next day, or the day after that. Each day I
> shall wait an hour. Au revoir, Louis Riel!

RIEL:

> Adieu, Uncle Gabriel!

Scene Sixteen

DUMONT:

> The next three days I stayed in the woods around
> Batoche. I hid my wife, and with my brother Elie
> I killed a cow for the women and children who had
> fled from the village, and we gathered hay to cover
> them. I saw the bare feet of the children, and I made
> them shoes out of rawhide. Our women were brave —
> braver than some of the men — and they laughed at
> their predicament. Every day I went looking for Riel,
> though my wife begged me to ride south and cross
> the border into safety. But I could not leave until
> I knew what had happened to my unfortunate friend.
> Three days I looked for him, and each evening I
> returned to the wood where we had parted. He was
> never there, and the next morning I said goodbye to
> my wife and my father, and I rode to the same wood
> on the last chance of seeing him.

> *The sound of horses' hooves crackling on
> woodland debris is heard.*

DUMAS:
Gabriel Dumont!

DUMONT:
Who is it? Is it you, Riel?

DUMAS:
It is Michel Dumas. Riel is not in a position to answer you, Gabriel.

DUMONT:
They have caught him?

DUMAS:
He gave himself up. We have destroyed him, Gabriel. We should never have asked him to come here.

DUMONT:
If we had not asked him he would have died with the thought in his mind that his mission was not fulfilled. He had the chance to go away three days ago when I invited him. He has decided to stay, and it is not our choice, but his.

DUMAS:
Are you going now?

DUMONT:
If Louis has surrendered, there is no reason to stay.

DUMAS:
May I come with you?

DUMONT:
Have you a rifle?

DUMAS:
I lost it when we ran away from the Gatling gun.

DUMONT:

> I still have my famous rifle, and Le Petit will shoot men and game for both of us. Have you any food? That is more important.

DUMAS:

> Six galettes. Nothing else.

DUMONT:

> Six dry cakes! So that is what we are left with after all our expectations and our efforts! Never mind — six dry cakes will take us as free men to the border.